Constitutional Law Outline

for the

Fourth and Fifth Amendments

of the

United States Constitution

D1563397

CONSTITUTIONAL LAW OUTLINE

FOR THE

FOURTH AND FIFTH AMENDMENTS

OF THE

UNITED STATES CONSTITUTION

DAN S. MURRELL

CAROLINA ACADEMIC PRESS

DURHAM, NORTH CAROLINA

ISBN 0-89089-868-5
LCCN 96-83984

Carolina Academic Press
700 Kent Street
Durham, North Carolina 27701
Telephone (919) 489-7486
Fax (919) 493-5668

Printed in the United States of America

Contents

v

FIFTH AMENDMENT RIGHTS OF THE ACCUSED

Acknowledgments

I am grateful for the assistance provided me over the years in developing this outline and wish to thank my graduate assistant Cathy Cubbon and those who preceded her, Jill Richey Rayburn, Robert B. Gaia, Lisa K. Coleman, Ben Wages, and Rebecca Snider. Their editorial and research work has been invaluable.

TABLE OF CASES

Constitutional Law Outline

for the

Fourth and Fifth Amendments

of the

United States Constitution

Arrest, Search & Seizure, and Warrants

1. Stop and Frisk

When may a law enforcement officer legally stop an individual for investigative purposes?

A law enforcement officer may stop an individual for investigative purposes and may detain the individual for a brief but reasonable period to determine whether or not a crime is about to be, is being, or has been committed.[1]

When may a law enforcement officer legally frisk an individual?

Incident to any stop or investigative delay, a law enforcement officer may frisk the individual stopped, if the officer has reason to believe that the person may be armed or is dangerous.[2] This is known as a "protective pat down."

What may a law enforcement officer seize during a protective pat down?

An officer may seize any contraband he discovers during a "Terry frisk" so long as the incriminating character of the contraband is "immediately apparent" to the officer. This only applies within the parameters of a "Terry frisk" for weapons. If the officer exceeds the bounds of *Terry*, then the

---

1. Terry v. Ohio, 392 U.S. 1 (1986).
2. *Id.*

seizure is constitutionally infirm.[3] This so called "plain feel" exception to the warrant requirement is based on the fact that the suspect's privacy interests are not advanced by excluding the contraband detected by touch. The officer has a legitimate right to frisk the suspect under *Terry*, thus excluding the results of the frisk would be pointless.

Investigatory Stops

What is an investigative detention?

Investigatory detentions involve reasonably brief encounters in which a reasonable person would believe that he or she is not free to leave, and in order to justify such Fourth Amendment seizures in these circumstances, the government must show a reasonable and articulable suspicion that the person has committed, is committing, or is about to commit a crime.[4]

Is there a test to determine if a person is seized?

The test is whether a reasonable man, viewing the particular police conduct as a whole and within the setting of all the surrounding circumstances, would conclude that the police have in some way restrained his liberty so that he was not free to leave.[5]

In order for a seizure of the person to have occurred, there must be either some application of physical force, even if extremely slight, or a show of authority to which the subject submits. A show of authority, without any application of physical force and to which the subject does not yield, is not a "seizure."[6] A police officer's actions of parking behind a

---

3. Minnesota v. Dickerson, 508 U.S. 366 , 113 S.Ct. 2130 (1993).
4. United States v. Hastamorir, 881 F.2d 1551 (11th Cir. 1989).
5. Michigan v. Chesternut, 486 U.S. 567 (1988).
6. California v. Hodari, 499 U.S. 621 (1991).

car in a parking area, asking the suspect to get into the patrol car, and withholding the suspect's identification and rental car agreement was held to constitute a seizure.[7] Police officers' actions in retaining an airline ticket and driver's license and asking the suspect to accompany them to a police room at an airport has also been considered a seizure.[8]

What is the level of suspicion needed to make a stop?

A law enforcement officer may make an investigatory stop of a suspicious individual to maintain the status quo while obtaining more information, even though the officer lacks probable cause to arrest the individual.[9] Reasonable suspicion is required for the initial detention and may not be subsequently developed from information obtained during the stop.[10]

"Reasonable suspicion" entails some minimal level of objective justification for making a stop, that is, something more than an inchoate or unparticularized suspicion or hunch, but less than the level of suspicion required for probable cause.[11] The assessment of particularized suspicion must be made based upon all the circumstances, including common sense conclusions about human behavior, that the person to be stopped is engaged in wrongdoing.[12] In assessing whether the grounds for a stop are adequate, the court should not ignore the considerable expertise that police have gained from their experience and training.[13] Thus, articulable suspicion may be based on the suspect's consistency with a

---

7. United States v. Jefferson, 906 F.2d 346 (8th Cir. 1990).

8. Florida v. Royer, 460 U.S. 491 (1983).

9. United States v. Jaccobs, 715 F.2d 1343 (Cal. Ct. App. 1983).

10. United States v. Jefferson, 906 F.2d 346 (8th Cir. 1990).

11. United States v. Sokolow, 490 U.S. 1 (1989).

12. United States v. Cortez, 449 U.S. 411 (1981).

13. United States v. McDonald, 670 F.2d 910 (10th Cir. 1982).

"profile" of criminal behavior.[14] However, there must be a reasonable basis for suspecting the particular person.[15]

What may provide reasonable suspicion for stopping a vehicle?

A finding of reasonable suspicion must be based upon the degree of suspicion that attaches to the circumstances of a particular stop, and not merely recitation of previously approved suspicious circumstances.[16]

The combination of an anonymous tip and a police officer's corroboration of some of the tip's details provide reasonable suspicion for stopping a vehicle.[17]

A driver of a vehicle may be ordered out when stopped for speeding, but a reasonable suspicion of the violation of a law is needed to order a passenger out of a vehicle.[18]

Reasonable suspicion, rather than probable cause, is sufficient to perform a roadside sobriety test if the driver is reasonably believed to be drinking.[19]

How long may a person be detained in an investigative detention?

An investigatory detention must be temporary and last no longer than is necessary to effectuate the purpose of the stop. Similarly, the investigative methods employed should be the least intrusive means which are reasonably available to verify or dispel the officer's suspicion.[20]

Inquiries made during investigatory stops need not always be limited to one or two questions; police may ask the de-

---

14. United States v. Sokolow, 490 U.S. 1 (1989).
15. United States v. Rodriguez, 976 F.2d 592 (9th Cir. 1992).
16. *Id.*
17. Alabama v. White, 496 U.S. 325 (1990).
18. Iowa v. Becker, 458 N.W.2d 604 (Iowa 1990).
19. Connecticut v. Lamme, 579 A.2d 484 (Conn. 1990).
20. Florida v. Royer, 460 U.S. 491 (1983).

tainee to explain suspicious circumstances, and the stop need not always be terminated within a couple of minutes, provided the scope of the inquiry and duration of the stop is reasonable and not excessive.[21]

Are all police encounters initiated by law enforcement officers' stops?

A stop is not necessarily implicated when a police officer initiates an encounter with a citizen whom the police officer has no articulable suspicion to suspect of criminal activity.[22] Officers, even without reasonable suspicion, may ask questions and request consent to search an individual's belongings, as long as the individual knows that compliance is not required.[23] However, for such an encounter to ripen into a stop, reasonable and articulable suspicion is required.[24]

Must the law enforcement officer provide Miranda warnings to the person stopped?

Miranda warnings are unnecessary for persons detained in "*Terry*" type stops.[25]

May a stop result in an arrest?

Founded suspicion to stop for investigatory detention may ripen into probable cause for arrest through the occurrence of facts or incidents after the stop.[26]

Does founded suspicion serve to justify a resultant arrest?

If the totality of circumstances—including the blocking of an individual's path, a display of weapons, the number of of-

---

21. United States v. Bautista, 684 F.2d 1286 (9th Cir. 1982).
22. United States v. Winston, 892 F.2d 112 (D.C. Ct. App. 1989).
23. Florida v. Bostick, 501 U.S. 429 (1991).
24. United States v. Wilson, 895 F.2d 168 (Va. Ct. App. 1960).
25. United States v. McGauley, 786 F.2d 888 (8th Cir. 1986).
26. United States v. Medina-Gasca, 739 F.2d 1451 (9th Cir. 1984).

ficers present and their demeanor, and the extent to which the officers physically restrain the individual—indicates that an encounter has become too intrusive to be classified as an investigatory detention, then the encounter is a full-scale arrest, and the government must establish that the arrest was supported by probable cause.[27]

Is the Fourth Amendment applicable to stops?

The Fourth Amendment applies to seizures of the person, including brief investigatory stops.[28] However, the Fourth Amendment does not apply to evidence discarded by the suspect prior to the seizure, and may be used at trial even if the subsequent stop was made without reasonable suspicion.[29]

Force

May an officer use force to effect a stop?

A valid stop is not transformed into an arrest because the police officer momentarily restricts a person's freedom of movement. Use of force in making a stop will not convert the stop into an arrest if it occurs under circumstances justifying the officer's fear for personal safety.[30]

Frisk

What is a frisk (pat down)?

A frisk is a pat down of the outer clothing to look for weapons. It is not a search, nor does it permit an intrusion beyond the needs of the frisk. The officer may, however, seize

---

27. United States v. Hastamorir, 881 F.2d 1551 (11th Cir. 1989).
28. United States v. Cortez, 449 U.S. 411 (1981).
29. California v. Hodari, 499 U.S. 621 (1991).
30. United States v. Jaccobs, 715 F.2d 1343 (Cal. Ct. App. 1983).

any items of contraband or evidence of a crime discovered by the senses of touch or sight incident to the lawful frisk.[31]

Must the officer feel fear to conduct a frisk (pat down)?

A policeman need not feel "scared" by the threat of danger to justify a stop and frisk. Evidence that the officer was aware of specific facts suggesting that the officer is in danger is sufficient to meet the constitutional requirements.[32] The constitutional basis of the *Terry* stop and frisk is the policy that the officer should be allowed to conduct a brief frisk in order to insure his own safety.

What degree of fear must be present to conduct the frisk (pat down)?

A stop must be based on a reasonable suspicion of criminal activity, and a frisk must be supported by a reasonable fear for the safety of the officer or others.[33]

A police officer is justified in conducting a pat down if he reasonably suspects that the person he has legitimately stopped is armed.[34]

What is the Plain Feel Doctrine?

If, during the course of a *Terry* protective patdown, an officer feels an object which he immediately recognizes as a contraband object by its mass or contour, the officer may seize the object, because there had been no additional invasion of privacy above or beyond that authorized by the officer's search for weapons.

However, this is a limited doctrine and, just as in plain view, the officer must have probable cause to believe that the object is contraband before seizing it. The officer may not ex-

---

31. Terry v. Ohio, 392 U.S. 1 (1968).
32. United States v. Thorpe, 536 F.2d 1098 (5th Cir. 1976).
33. United States v. Hammack, 604 F.2d 437 (Tex. Ct. App. 1979).
34. United States v. Gonzalez Athehorta, 729 F. Supp. 248 (E.D.N.Y. 1990).

ceed the bounds of *Terry* to establish this probable cause. The officer may not find probable cause by "squeezing, sliding and otherwise manipulating" the object.[35]

2. Arrest, Search and Seizure

Seizure

What is a seizure?

A seizure occurs when there is some meaningful interference with an individual's possessory interests in the property seized.[36]

Arrest

What is an arrest and a search?

An arrest occurs when a person is deprived of his or her freedom to come and go. A search occurs when an expectation of privacy, that society is prepared to consider as reasonable, is infringed.[37]

Probable Cause

Is there a standard for arrests?

Every arrest, and every seizure that has the attributes of a formal arrest, is unreasonable unless supported by probable cause.[38]

---

35. Minnesota v. Dickerson, 508 U.S. 366, 113 S. Ct. 2130 (1993).
36. Maryland v. Macon, 472 U.S. 463 (1985); *see also*, Soldal v. Cook County, 113 S.Ct. 538 (1992).
37. Maryland v. Macon, 472 U.S. 463 (1985).
38. Michigan v. Summers, 452 U.S. 692 (D.C. Ct. App. 1981).

The touchstone of determining the legality of an arrest is whether the arresting officer had probable cause to believe a crime had been committed and that the arrested person committed it.[39]

Is probable cause sufficient guilt to convict a suspect?

It is not necessary that the arresting officer possess knowledge of facts sufficient to establish guilt; however, more than mere is suspicion is required.[40]

What level of information satisfies the probable cause requirement?

Collection of knowledge, rather than sole knowledge of any individual officer is a factor to be considered when determining the existence of probable cause to make an arrest.[41]

One officer may rely on information provided by another officer to establish founded suspicion or probable cause.[42]

Existence of probable cause to arrest must be based on the totality of circumstances, and where law enforcement authorities are cooperating in an investigation, knowledge of one is presumed shared by all.[43]

However, a supervising officer's knowledge about a defendant cannot be relied upon to provide probable cause for a defendant's arrest if there is no evidence that such knowledge was communicated to agents on the scene who actually made the arrest.[44]

---

39. United.States. v. Allen, 629 F.2d 51 (D.C. Ct. App. 1980).
40. United States v. Hansen, 652 F.2d 1374 (10th Cir. 1981).
41. United States v. Butler, 611 F.2d 1066 (5th Cir. 1980).
42. United States v. Burnette, 698 F.2d 1038 (9th Cir. 1983).
43. Calamia v. City of New York, 879 F.2d 1025 (7th Cir. 1989).
44. United States. v. Edwards, 885 F.2d 377 (7th Cir. 1989).

Arrest Warrants

Does a law enforcement officer need a warrant to arrest a suspected offender?

As a rule, a warrant should always be obtained if there is time.

Generally, a defendant may be arrested without a warrant only if probable cause exists at the time of arrest.[45]

When arrests are made in public places, an arrest warrant has never been considered constitutionally mandated, even when there was an opportunity for one to be obtained.[46]

An arrest may be made in a public place without a warrant,[47] and such arrests in public, with probable cause, do not violate the Fourth Amendment, even though exigent circumstances do not exist.[48] After a warrantless arrest, however, a probable cause determination must be made[49] no more than 48 hours after the arrest.[50]

Law enforcement officers may make a warrantless arrest in exigent circumstances, such as when a suspect may flee or destroy evidence.[51]

A warrantless arrest is valid if supported by probable cause. The determination of the existence of probable cause is a mixed question of fact and law in which legal issues predominate and is therefore "...subject to *de novo* review," but the underlying facts as found by the district court are reviewed for clear error.[52]

---

45. United States. v. Porter, 701 F.2d 1158 (6th Cir. 1983).
46. United States v. Fernandez-Guzman, 577 F.2d 1093 (7th Cir. 1978).
47. United States v. Bush , 647 F.2d 357 (3d Cir. 1981).
48. United States v. Maez, 872 F.2d 1444 (10th Cir. 1989).
49. Gerstein v. Pugh, 420 U.S. 103 (1975).
50. County of Riverside v. McLaughlin, 500 U.S. 44 (1991).
51. United States v. Clark, 754 F.2d 789 (8th Cir. 1985).
52. United States v. Hoyos, 892 F.2d 1387 (9th Cir. 1989).

The burden of proving the legality of a challenged warrantless arrest rests upon the government.[53]

Are any areas protected from warrantless arrests?

The Fourth Amendment prohibits the police from making warrantless and non-consensual entry into a suspect's home in order to make a routine felony arrest.[54]

By retreating into a private place (a home), a defendant cannot thwart an otherwise proper arrest that had been set in motion in a public place.

If there is a need for the police to act quickly to prevent the destruction of evidence and there is a true "hot pursuit," the warrantless entry by the police into the house to make the arrest is justified.[55]

How soon must an officer armed with a warrant carry out an arrest?

The general rule is that, while the execution of an arrest warrant should not be unreasonably delayed, law enforcement officers have a reasonable time in which to execute a warrant, and need not make the arrest at the first opportunity.[56]

Valid Arrests

What makes an arrest valid?

The motivation of a police officer is a key element to the constitutionality of an arrest. If the arrest is pretextual, that is, if it appears to be for a traffic violation but is really for an

53. United States v. Allen, 629 F.2d 51 (D.C. Ct. App. 1980).
54. Payton v. New York, 445 U.S. 573 (1980).
55. United States v. Santana, 427 U.S. 38 (1976).
56. United States v. Drake, 655 F.2d 1025 (10th Cir. 1981).

ulterior purpose, such as illegally searching the car, then the arrest is unconstitutional.[57]

The "high crime" character of an area may be a relevant factor in determining probable cause to arrest or search.[58]

However, the mere fact that a defendant is in the company of a person whom the police had probable cause to arrest does not establish probable cause to arrest the defendant.[59]

Where an arrest is based on the good faith enforcement of a previously valid regulation, including regulations issued by the various branches of the armed forces, such an arrest is not invalid if the regulation is later declared unconstitutional.[60]

Force

What force may law enforcement officers use in effecting an arrest?

A law enforcement officer is never justified in effecting an arrest by use of excessive force.

In order to keep within the confines of the Eighth and Fourteenth Amendments, only force that is necessary and reasonable under the circumstances is proper.

Theoretically, no force may be expended if the arrestee submits to arrest.[61]

When a police officer has probable cause to believe that a criminal suspect possesses a threat of serious physical harm, either to the officer or others, it is not constitutionally unreasonable to prevent escape by use of deadly force, and if, where feasible, some warning has been given.[62] In making an

---

57. Donaldson v. Hovanec, 473 F. Supp. 602 (E.D. Pa 1979).
58. United States v. White, 655 F.2d 1302 (D.C. Ct. App. 1981).
59. United States v. Capers, 685 F.2d 249 (8th Cir. 1982).
60. Boeckenhaupt v. United States, 537 F.2d 1182 (4th Cir. 1976).
61. Moats v. Village of Schaumburg, 562 F. Supp. 624 (N.D. Ill. 1983).
62. Tennessee v. Garner, 471 U.S. 1 (1985).

arrest, an officer has the right to use some degree of physical coercion or threat to effect the arrest. Whether the force used in making the arrest was unreasonable is to be determined in light of all the circumstances, including the severity of the crime at issue and whether the suspect poses immediate threat to the safety of the officers or others or actively resists arrest or attempts to flee.

Reasonableness must be judged from the perspective of a reasonable officer on the scene, rather than by hindsight.[63]

Does the constitution provide any limits on the officer when he or she effects an arrest?

The function of police or other law enforcement officers in making an arrest is not to determine guilt or inflict punishment, but merely to apprehend suspects and arrange for their appearance in due course before the adjudicating agency.[64]

What law applies when an officer of one jurisdiction effects an arrest for a crime of another jurisdiction?

When a state officer makes an arrest for a federal crime, the legality of the arrest is determined by the law of the state in which the arrest occurs, subject to federal constitutional standards.[65]

Fifth Amendment Rights Affecting Arrest, Search, and Seizure

What is a Miranda warning and when is it required?

A *Miranda* warning is required prior to custodial interrogation and is a warning that the suspect has a right to remain

63. Zuchel v. Spinharney, 890 F.2d 273 (10th Cir. 1989).
64. Samuel v. Busnuck, 423 F. Supp. 99 (D.C. Md. 1976).
65. United States v. Taylor, 797 F.2d 1563 (11th Cir. 1986).

silent, a right to counsel, and that his statements may be used as evidence against him. This right may be voluntarily waived, or may be invoked at any stage of the questioning.[66] The *Miranda* requirement is dispensed with in only a few circumstances. One such exception to the general rule is for a law enforcement officer acting as an inmate, who need not uncover his or her identity by giving *Miranda* warnings to a jail suspect before asking questions that may elicit an incriminating response regarding an uncharged crime.[67] Also, police officers are not required to give *Miranda* warnings before asking questions that are not incriminating, such as name and address, nor for eliciting nontestimonial responses, such as submitting a suspect to a sobriety test.[68]

When is a person in custody for purposes of Miranda?

The standard is an objective view of the circumstances surrounding the interrogation. The subjective views of the officer and the person being interrogated are irrelevant.[69]

May police interrogate a charged defendant who has requested counsel?

Police may not interrogate a formally charged defendant that has requested counsel until counsel is made available to him, unless the suspect himself initiates further communication with officers.[70] Nor may officials reinitiate interrogation of an accused without counsel present after the accused has requested and been provided counsel. The Fifth Amendment protection is not terminated or suspended when the suspect has consulted with an attorney.[71] Even if the reinitiation of

---

66. Miranda v. Arizona, 384 U.S. 436 (1966).
67. Illinois v. Perkins, 496 U.S. 292 (1990).
68. Pennsylvania v. Muniz, 496 U.S. 582 (1990).
69. Stansbury v. California, 114 S. Ct. 1526 (1994).
70. Edwards. v. Arizona, 451 U.S. 477 (1981).
71. Minnick v. Mississippi, 498 U.S. 146 (1990).

interrogation concerns a different offense or involves different law enforcement officers, statements may not be taken without counsel present if the suspect has previously requested counsel.[72] This request for counsel must be unambiguous; stating, "Maybe I should talk to a lawyer" is not unambiguous and is, therefore, not sufficient to cause the officers to cease questioning the defendant without presence of counsel.[73]

Will statements obtained in violation of a suspect's Miranda rights be admissible at trial?

Any statements thus attained are not admissible at trial as evidence, but may be used to impeach a defendant.[74]

Does invocation of the Sixth Amendment right to counsel also invoke the Miranda right?

The Sixth Amendment right to counsel is offense-specific; therefore, the assertion of that right at a critical stage of the proceedings after charges have been filed does not invoke the Fifth Amendment based *Miranda* right to counsel during interrogation about unrelated offenses.[75] However, the assertion of the Sixth Amendment right to counsel does invoke the Miranda right to counsel during subsequent interrogation of that offense, even if a waiver is obtained before the subsequent interrogation.[76]

What are other considerations in eliciting incriminating responses from suspects?

A confession may not be coerced and the determination of coercion depends on the totality of the circumstances. Actual

---

72. Arizona v. Roberson, 486 U.S. 675 (1988).
73. Davis v. United States, 114 S. Ct. 2350 (1994).
74. Michigan v. Harvey, 494 U.S. 344 (1990).
75. McNeil v. Wisconsin, 501 U.S. 171 (1991).
76. Michigan v. Jackson, 475 U.S. 625 (1986).

violence by an officer is not required; a credible threat may be sufficient to find coercion. If a defendant's confession is coerced, its use against the defendant will not be allowed at trial. Upon appeal, if the trial court admits the evidence, that decision will be reviewed *de novo*, and may be held to be harmless error.[77]

An illegal warrantless entry pursuant to a routine felony arrest may taint an inculpatory statement, but if the statement was made outside the home following the arrest, and if the arrest was based on probable cause, it will be admissible.[78]

3. Search Warrants

Generally

What is a search warrant?

A warrant is a judicial order directing an officer or class of officers to conduct the search for the specified items or property. The purpose of a warrant is to allow a neutral judicial officer to assess whether police have probable cause to make an arrest or conduct a search.[79]

The Fourth Amendment envisioned the "judicial eye" looking over the law enforcement officer's shoulder.

A major function of a search warrant is to provide the property owner with sufficient information to assure him of the legality of the search.[80]

---

77. Arizona v. Fulminante, 499 U.S. 279 (1991).
78. New York v. Harris, 495 U.S. 14 (1990).
79. Steagald v. United States, 451 U.S. 204 (1981).
80. Michigan v. Tyler, 436 U.S. 499 (1978).

Permissible Objects

What may be searched for pursuant to a search warrant?

A state is not prohibited from issuing a warrant to search for evidence simply because the owner or possessor of the place or thing to be searched is not reasonably suspected of criminal involvement.[81]

Property owned by a person absolutely innocent of any wrongdoing may be searched under a valid warrant.[82]

Does a warrant authorize the search of a third-party home?

Police may not search the home of a third party, even when armed with a valid arrest warrant, for an individual who does not live on the premises searched.[83]

Sufficiency of Affidavit

What is required in an affidavit to obtain a warrant?

Affidavits in support of warrants are examined in a common sense and realistic manner.[84]

The validity of the warrant depends upon what is found within the four corners of the underlying affidavit.[85]

When acting with urgency and in good faith, government agents do not necessarily prejudice a defendant by tape-recording his affidavit, presenting it to the magistrate, and swearing to the truth of its contents, even though this is a violation of the rules of criminal procedure.[86]

---

81. Zurcher v. Stanford Daily, 436 U.S. 547 (1983).
82. United States v. Tehfe, 722 F.2d 1114 (3d Cir. 1983).
83. Steagald v. United States, 451 U.S. 204 (1981).
84. United States v. Crozier, 777 F.2d 1376 (9th Cir. 1985).
85. United States v. Taylor, 716 F.2d 701 (9th Cir. 1983).
86. United States v. Vassar, 648 F.2d 507 (9th Cir. 1980).

Must the affiant always be present before the magistrate?

Magistrates are often authorized to issue warrants based on telephone conversations.[87]

Inaccurate Statements

Must the assertions of the affiant or officers be accurate?

Insignificant or immaterial misrepresentations or omissions will not in and of themselves invalidate a search warrant.[88]

If at a preliminary hearing it is shown by a preponderance of the evidence that a intentional false statement, or one made with a reckless disregard for the truth, was included in a search warrant affidavit, and that with the affidavit's false statement set aside, the affidavit's remaining contents are insufficient to establish probable cause, then the search warrant must be voided and the fruits of the search excluded to the same extent as if probable cause was lacking on the face of the affidavit.[89]

Probable Cause

Is probable cause the same for a search warrant as for an arrest warrant?

Probable cause for issuance of a search warrant exists when, considering all of the circumstances, there is a fair probability that contraband or evidence of a crime will be found in a particular place.[90]

---

87. United States v. Cuaron, 700 F.2d 582 (10th Cir. 1983).
88. United States v. Ofshe, 817 F.2d 1508 (11th Cir. 1987).
89. Franks v. Delaware, 438 U.S. 152 (1978).
90. United States v. Pryor, 652 F. Supp. 1353 (D. Me. 1987).

Upon what is probable cause based?

While a search warrant affidavit must be true, that does not mean truthful in that every fact recited in the warrant affidavit is necessarily correct. Probable cause may be founded on hearsay and upon information received from informants, as well as upon information within the affiant's own knowledge that sometimes must be garnered hastily. Again, hearsay evidence may be used to establish probable cause.[91]

The affidavit is to be truthful in that the information put forth is believed or appropriately accepted by the affiant as true.[92]

To determine whether an affidavit is sufficient to support a finding of probable cause, a "totality of circumstances" approach is taken. A balanced assessment of the relevant weights of various indicia of reliability, including the affiant's veracity and basis of his knowledge as set forth in the affidavit, are to be considered.[93]

Simply stated, probable cause is more reason to believe than not that the evidence sought for a particular crime will be found as stated.

Informants

May informants be used to support search warrants?

"Totality of circumstances" is the prevailing test for determining whether an informant's tip suffices to establish probable cause for the issuance of a search warrant.[94]

---

91. United States v. McCoy, 781 F.2d 168 (10th Cir. 1985).
92. United States v. Torres, 583 F. Supp. 86 (N.D. Ill. 1984).
93. United States v. Griffin, 827 F.2d 1108 (7th Cir. 1987).
94. United States v. Leon, 468 U.S. 897 (1984).

Are there concerns with the informant's credibility?

An informant's credibility may be established by a search warrant affidavit's recitation of the informant's past instances of reliability.[95]

Although there is no specific test regarding the veracity of an informant, some evidence bearing on the informant's reliability must be presented to the magistrate.[96]

It has been held on at least one occasion that a probable cause affidavit stating that the police officer received information from an informant, who was known to the officer and who had provided past information leading to arrests and convictions, is a "bare bones" affidavit, constitutionally defective, and does not justify the officer's good faith reliance thereon.[97]

May anonymous tips be utilized?

To assess probable cause for the issuance of a search warrant based on an anonymous tip, it is sufficient to corroborate that tip with other independent sources of information.[98]

A tip from an unfamiliar informant is generally insufficient to support a finding of probable cause. However, reliability may be established by independent means such as a search warrant affidavit's recitation of the informant's past instances of reliability.[99]

---

95. United States v. White, 704 F. Supp. 90 (E.D. N.C. 1989).
96. United States v. Schwimmer, 692 F. Supp. 119 (E.D.N.Y. 1988).
97. United States v. Barrington, 806 F.2d 529 (5th Cir. 1986).
98. Illinois v. Gates, 462 U.S. 213 (1983).
99. United States v. White, 704 F. Supp. 90 (E.D. N.C. 1989).

Application and Staleness

Must warrants be sought in a timely manner?

Delay in seeking a search warrant may invalidate the warrant because probable cause must exist at the time the warrant is issued, not earlier. Lapse of time is not necessarily the controlling factor. Other factors include the nature of the criminal activity and type of property sought, viewed in light of common sense.[100]

The probable cause standard is not satisfied if the government can establish only that the items to be seized could have been found at a certain location some time in the past. Rather, the government must reveal facts that make it likely that the items being sought are in a certain place when the warrant issues.[101]

Contraband does not have to be presently located at the place described in a warrant if there is probable cause to believe that the contraband will be there when the warrant in executed.[102]

Where information points to illegal activity of a continuous nature, the passage of several months between observations in the search warrant affidavit and issuance of the warrant will not render the information stale.[103]

Content

What information must the search warrant contain?

Search warrants are not normally directed at persons. They authorize a search of "places" and a seizure of "things"

---

100. United States v. Ellison, 793 F.2d 942 (8th Cir. 1986).
101. United States v. Domme, 753 F.2d 950 (11th Cir. 1985).
102. United States v. Lowe, 575 F.2d 1193 (6th Cir. 1978).
103. United States v. Hershenow, 680 F.2d 847 (1st Cir. 1982).

and, as a constitutional matter, need not even name the person from whom things will be seized.[104]

Inadequacies in description in search warrants cannot be cured by reference to an affidavit that was neither attached to the warrant nor incorporated by reference.[105]

A warrant must particularly describe the things to be seized and is intended to prevent a general exploratory rummaging in a person's belongings.[106]

Particularity

How specific must a warrant be?

Should a warrant turn out to be ambiguous in scope, its validity must be judged in light of the information available to the officer at the time the warrant was obtained. The discovery of facts demonstrating that an otherwise valid warrant was unnecessarily broad does not retroactively invalidate the warrant.[107]

A warrant's description of items need only be reasonably specific, rather than elaborately detailed.[108] A search warrant may contain a catchall phrase as long as it sufficiently limits the discretion of the officers who execute the warrant.[109]

A search warrant written in boiler plate terms, without explicit limitations on the scope of the search, with only a description of a crime and without limitation on the kind of evidence sought, is impermissibly broad.[110]

To the extent that a search warrant specifically lists types of evidence to be seized, it is not overly broad. To the extent

---

104. Zurcher v. Stanford Daily, 436 U.S. 547 (1978).
105. United States v. Stubbs, 873 F.2d 210 (9th Cir. 1989).
106. Coolidge v. New Hampshire, 403 U.S. 443 (1971).
107. Maryland v. Garrison, 480 U.S. 79 (1987).
108. United States v. Holzeman, 871 F.2d 1496 (9th Cir. 1989).
109. United States v. Brown, 832 F.2d 991 (7th Cir. 1987).
110. United States v. Buck, 813 F.2d 588 (2d Cir. 1987).

that material outside the specifically listed types of evidence are seized, suppression may be ordered as to that evidence without requiring the suppression of all evidence seized.[111]

A warrant should be specific enough so that the officer or officers to whom it is directed can, without more, carry out the purpose of the warrant. It must be broad enough to complete the search without allowing random "shopping" for evidence.

Execution

May an officer use force to execute a search warrant?

An officer may use the minimum force necessary to carry out the dictates of the warrant. Any destruction caused by law enforcement officers in the execution of a search or arrest warrant must be necessary to effectively execute the warrant.[112]

Who may execute a search warrant?

A search warrant may be executed by persons to whom the search warrant is directed or by any officer authorized by law to execute search warrants.[113]

Must officers always knock and announce their purpose when executing a search warrant?

Officers may be excused from announcing the purpose of their search warrant when they reasonably believe that the persons to be apprehended might destroy evidence during the delay in police entry.[114]

Exigent circumstances may excuse non-compliance with the knock-and-announce rule only where officers believe that

---

111. United States v. Coleman, 805 F.2d 474 (3d Cir. 1986).
112. Ginter v. Stallcup, 869 F.2d 384 (8th Cir. 1989).
113. United States v. Ofshe, 817 F.2d 1508 (11th Cir. 1987).
114. United States v. Tracy, 835 F.2d 1267 (8th Cir. 1988).

there is an emergency situation, and when that belief is objectively reasonable.[115]

Are nighttime searches allowed?

The rule prohibiting nighttime searches is violated only if, either intentionally or with reckless disregard for the truth, the information necessary to determine probable cause for the nighttime search is omitted from the warrant application.[116]

What may be searched under the search warrant?

Police may search all items which legitimately might contain objects specified in the search warrant.[117]

It seems appropriate to note the "elephant rule;"[118] that is if the officer is looking for an elephant, he or she may search only were they would expect to find an elephant. As an example, the freezing compartment of a refrigerator would be out of bounds for a legitimate search if searching for an elephant. Conversely, if the officer is looking for drugs, the search is broadened and he or she may look where the drugs may be found, i.e., in the freezing compartment or in the garage. This is particularly important should the officers discover, in plain view, items suspected of being evidence of another crime.

---

115. United States v. Spinelli, 848 F.2d 26 (2d Cir. 1988).
116. United States v. Pryor, 652 F. Supp 1353 (D. Me. 1987).
117. United States v. Disla, 805 F.2d 1340 (9th Cir. 1986).
118. I created the "elephant rule" to emphasize the point that an officer may seize evidence only if he or she is where he or she has a right to be and is looking in a place in which the specified evidence may be found.

4. Warrantless Searches and Seizures

When is a suspect "seized"?

A suspect is "seized" only if, under all the circumstances a reasonable person would believe he was not free to leave. No seizure occurs when a law enforcement officer attempts to apprehend a suspect by a show of authority, but the suspect does not submit.[119] However, restraint by physical force is a seizure.

When may a warrantless seizure occur?

Police may only arrest a suspect upon a showing of probable cause. If because of exigent circumstances no warrant is available, police may arrest a suspect if they have a reasonable belief the suspect is engaged in, or has committed a crime. The information required to support a showing of probable cause can be satisfied by an informants' tip.[120]

The informants' veracity, reliability, and any independent corroboration obtained by the officers are relevant factors to a judicial determination of probable cause.[121]

May consent justify a search in lieu of a search warrant?

A warrantless entry and search by law enforcement officers does not violate the Fourth Amendment's proscription against unreasonable searches and seizures if the officers have obtained the consent of the owner or a third party who possesses common authority over the premises.[122] However, consent obtained after an illegal entry does not justify the entry.[123]

---

119. United States v. Mendenhall, 446 U.S. 544 (1980).
120. California v. Hodari, 499 U.S. 621 (1991).
121. Illinois v. Gates, 462 U.S. 213 (1983).
122. United States v. Matlock, 415 U.S. 164 (1974).
123. United States v. Duchi, 906 F.2d 1278 (11th Cir. 1989).

A warrantless entry is valid when based upon the consent of a third party whom the police, at the time of the entry, reasonably believe to possess common authority over the premises, even though the party in fact does not.[124]

The warrantless videotaping of a criminal act with a hidden camera in a home based on the consent of an inhabitant, is nonetheless unconstitutional when a cohabitant is videotaped while the consenting inhabitant is away from the premises.[125]

Are guests without the right of privacy in a host's home?

A person's status as an overnight guest is sufficient to show that he has an expectation of privacy in the home that society recognizes as reasonable. Under the Fourth Amendment, an overnight guest has standing to challenge the legality of a warrantless entry in the home to effect his arrest.[126]

Are there other grounds for a warrantless search?

Warrantless searches and seizures of abandoned property do not violate the Fourth Amendment;[127] therefore, the warrantless search and seizure of garbage bags left for collection outside the curtilage of the home is permissible, according to the Supreme Court.[128] However, some state supreme courts construe their state constitutions more strictly, requiring a warrant to search garbage placed outside the dwelling for collection.[129]

The risk of loss of evidence may also justify a warrantless entry, but not if the risk was caused by the actions of the officers.[130]

---

124. Illinois v. Rodriguez, 497 U.S. 177 (1990).
125. California v. Henderson, 220 Cal. App.3d 1632 (4th Cir. 1990).
126. Minnesota v. Olson, 495 U.S. 91(1990).
127. United States v. Thomas, 864 F.2d 843 (D.C. Ct. App. 1989).
128. California v. Greenwood, 486 U.S. 35 (1988).
129. *See, e.g.,* New Jersey v. Hempele, 576 A.2d 793 (N.J. 1990).
130. United States v. Duchi, 906 F.2d 1278 (8th Cir. 1990).

Does the Fourth Amendment apply to foreign residences?

The Fourth Amendment only applies to United States citizens or persons who have developed a significant connection with the United States to be considered a part of it; therefore, the Fourth Amendment does not apply to searches and seizures of the residences of foreign nationals located in foreign countries.[131]

Exclusionary Rule

May evidence seized illegally be used at trial?

Evidence obtained from an illegal search may not be used as evidence against the defendant at trial.[132] However, defendants may be impeached using the illegally obtained evidence under an exception to the exclusionary rule.[133] Other defense witnesses may not be impeached using the illegally obtained evidence.[134]

Are there exceptions to the exclusionary rule?

If officers rely in good faith upon a search warrant in obtaining evidence, the Fourth Amendment does not preclude its use at trial, even if the warrant is subsequently found to be unsupported by probable cause.[135] However, some state courts do not apply this good faith exception to the exclusionary rule.[136]

Evidence discovered during the execution of a valid search warrant will not be suppressed due to its observance during a prior illegal entry, if the probable cause to support the war-

---

131. United States v. Verdugo-Uriquidez, 494 U.S. 259 (1990).
132. Mapp v. Ohio, 367 U.S. 643 (1961).
133. Walder v. United States, 347 U.S. 62 (1954).
134. James v. Illinois, 493 U.S. 307 (1990).
135. United States v. Leon, 468 U.S. 897 (1984).
136. Connecticut v. Morrisey, 579 A.2d 58 (Conn. 1990).

rant is on the basis of information obtained through an independent source and not during the prior entry.[137] Some states allow an inevitable discovery exception to the exclusionary rule in certain circumstances.

For example, illegally obtained evidence that would have inevitably been discovered during a vehicle inventory search may be admitted at trial, if the police can show that routine inventory procedures exist.[138]

May an interested third party assert another's Fourth Amendment right?

A co-conspirator does not have standing to assert the rights of another relative to an unconstitutional seizure.[139]

5. Vehicles

Lessened Expectation of Privacy

Are the standards for searching a vehicle different from other search areas?

Persons traveling in automobiles on public thoroughfares have no reasonable expectation of privacy in their movements from one place to another.[140]

The reasons for distinguishing between automobiles and homes or offices in relation to the Fourth Amendment are two-fold:

First, the inherent mobility of automobiles creates circumstances of such exigency that, as a practical necessity, rigorous enforcement of the warrant requirement is impossible.

---

137. Murray v. United States, 487 U.S. 533 (1988).
138. Missouri v. Milliorn, 794 S.W.2d 181 (Mo. 1990).
139. United States v. Padilla, 507 U.S. 904, 113 S.Ct. 1936 (1993).
140. United States v. Knotts, 460 U.S. 276 (1983).

Warrantless searches may be upheld even if there is no immediate danger of the automobile being removed from the jurisdiction.

Second, less rigorous warrant requirements govern because the expectation of privacy in an automobile is significantly less than the expectation of privacy in one's home or office.[141]

There is no legitimate expectation of privacy in any portion of an automobile visible from the outside. A right of privacy is not violated when an officer looks through a vehicle's windows.[142]

An individual's expectation of privacy in his automobile is less than in any other property.[143]

Obviously an officer would be wise to seek a warrant, even when dealing with vehicles, if there is time.

Probable Cause for Vehicle Search

What is probable cause for a vehicle search without a warrant?

It is axiomatic that searches conducted outside the judicial process without prior approval by a judge or magistrate are *per se* unreasonable. However, one of the few specifically established and well delineated exceptions to the warrant is that an automobile may be searched when police lawfully stop it and have probable cause to believe that it contains evidence of crime.[144]

"Probable cause to search a vehicle" exists when facts and circumstances would lead a reasonably prudent person to believe that the vehicle contains contraband. To determine

---

141. South Dakota v. Opperman, 428 U.S. 364 (1976).
142. Brumfield v. Jones, 849 F.2d 152 (5th Cir. 1988).
143. United States v. Michael, 645 F.2d 252 (11th Cir. 1981).
144. Colorado v. Bannister, 449 U.S. 1 (1980).

whether probable cause exists, the court examines the totality of circumstances and inferences that flow therefrom.[145]

What are the limits of a search based on probable cause?

If probable cause justifies the search of a lawfully stopped automobile, it justifies the search of every part of the vehicle and any contents that may conceal the object of the search.[146]

When an officer has probable cause to believe contraband exists anywhere in an automobile, he may search for it and seize it. [147]

If the requirements for a warrantless search of an automobile were met at the time the automobile was stopped, the police may, as an alternate to a contemporaneous search, seize the car, return it to police headquarters, and search it there.[148]

Exigent circumstances justifying a warrantless automobile search include those which indicate that the automobile cannot be adequately secured while a warrant is being obtained.[149]

Scope of Vehicle Search

What is the scope of the warrantless vehicle search?

The scope of a warrantless search of an automobile is as extensive as a magistrate could legitimately authorize by warrant.[150]

Police who have legitimately stopped an automobile and who have probable cause to believe that contraband is con-

---

145. United States v. Alexander, 835 F.2d 1406 (11th Cir. 1988).
146. United States v. Ross, 456 U.S. 790 (1982).
147. United States v. Boden, 854 F.2d 983 (7th Cir. 1988).
148. United States v. Thomas, 536 F. Supp. 736 (D.C. Ala. 1982).
149. Id.
150. United States v. Prati, 861 F.2d 82 (5th Cir. 1988).

cealed within the car may make a probing search of compartments and containers.[151]

Police who have probable cause to search either an entire vehicle or a container located within may search that container. However, if the probable cause pertains to the container only, the entire vehicle may not be searched.[152]

Police officers who have probable cause to believe that an automobile contains evidence of crime may search the vehicle, including the trunk and all containers in which there is probable cause to believe that evidence is concealed.[153]

Police officers may search a vehicle if the owner or apparent owner consents and has the knowledge that he or she does not have to consent to the search. If consent to search the vehicle is obtained, closed containers within the vehicle that could contain the object of the search may also be searched, but a warrant should be obtained to search locked or sealed containers unless separate consent is given to search them.[154]

Inventory Searches

What is the purpose of an inventory of a vehicle taken into police custody?

The routine practice of securing and inventorying the contents of an impounded automobile was developed in response to three distinct needs:

(1) the protection of the owner's property while it remains in police custody;

(2) protection of police against claims or disputes about lost or stolen property;

---

151. United States v. Parr, 843 F.2d 1228 (9th Cir. 1988).
152. California v. Acevedo, 500 U.S. 565 (1991).
153. United States v. Alvarez, 899 F.2d 833 (9th Cir. 1990).
154. Florida v. Jimeno, 500 U.S. 248 (1991).

(3) protection of police from potential danger.

Also, such practices are viewed as essential to respond to incidents of theft or vandalism, and in determining whether a vehicle has been stolen or abandoned.[155]

Does the warrant requirement of the Fourth Amendment apply to the inventory search?

Regarding non-investigative inventories of automobiles lawfully within police custody, the policies underlying the warrant requirement are inapplicable. Therefore, searches of lawfully impounded vehicles are reasonable and do not violate the Fourth Amendment.[156]

An inventory search will not be sustained when the court believes the police were rummaging through the automobile for incriminating evidence of other offenses.[157]

When police, in the exercise of the "community caretaking function," acquire temporary custody of a vehicle, a warrantless inventory search of the vehicle made pursuant to standard police procedures and for the purpose of securing and protecting the vehicle and its contents is a reasonable intrusion that does not offend the Fourth Amendment.[158]

Exigent circumstances that justify a warrantless vehicle search do not cease once police have impounded a car. Therefore, the search of a car subsequent to impoundment is not improper.[159]

May the inventory search extend to all areas of the vehicle?

The needs of the government in conducting an inventory search are ordinarily accomplished without intrusion into the

---

155. South Dakota v. Opperman, 428 U.S. 364 (1976).
156. Id.
157. United States v. Feldman, 788 F.2d 544 (9th Cir. 1986).
158. United States v. Staller, 616 F.2d 1284 (11th Cir. 1980).
159. United States v. Shaw, 701 F.2d 367 (5th Cir. 1983).

locked trunk of an automobile. Absent specific justification for a more extensive intrusion, the routine search of a locked trunk is unreasonable under the Fourth Amendment.[160]

May the inventory search extend into locked or sealed containers?

A police officer is not entitled to open locked suitcases found in an automobile during an inventory search when there exists no policy whatever regarding the opening of closed containers during such inventory searches. Absent such a policy, the search is not sufficiently regulated to satisfy the Fourth Amendment, and evidence of crime found in such containers is subject to suppression.[161]

The rule that standardized criteria, or an established routine, must regulate the opening of closed containers during inventory searches is based upon the principal that an inventory search cannot be used as a ruse for a general rummaging in order to discover incriminating evidence. The policy or practice governing inventory searches should be designed to produce an inventory. The individual police officer must not be allowed so much latitude that the inventory searches are reduced to purposeful and general means of discovering evidence of crime.[162]

While a policy of opening all containers or of opening no containers during an inventory search is permissible, it is equally permissible to allow police to open closed containers when the contents of the containers cannot be ascertained from an examination of the exterior of the container. To allow an exercise of judgment based on such concerns relating to an inventory search does not violate the Fourth Amendment.[163]

---

160. United States v. Wilson, 636 F.2d 1161 (8th Cir. 1980).
161. Florida v. Wells, 495 U.S. 1 (1990).
162. *Id.*
163. *Id.*

6. Plain View

What is the plain view doctrine?

The plain view doctrine permits the warrantless seizure by police of private possessions when three requirements are met:

First, the police must lawfully make an "initial intrusion" or otherwise properly be in a position from which a particular area can be viewed.

Second, the officer must discover the incriminating evidence inadvertently; in other words, he may not know in advance the location of certain evidence and then seize it, relying on the plain view doctrine only as a pretext.

Finally, it must be immediately apparent to the officer that the observed items may be evidence of a crime, contraband or otherwise subject to seizure.[164]

Does the Fourth Amendment allow the seizure of items in plain view?

The Fourth Amendment does not prohibit the warrantless seizure of evidence of crime in plain view; although inadvertence is characteristic of most plain view seizures, it is not a necessary condition.[165]

If a police officer has a valid warrant to search for one item, but merely a suspicion concerning another—whether or not the suspicion amounts to probable cause—the other item is not immunized from seizure if it is found during a lawful search for the first.[166]

---

164. Coolidge v. New Hampshire, 403 U.S. 443 (1971).
165. Horton v. California, 496 U.S. 128 (1990).
166. *Id.*

What must occur to allow a seizure under the plain view doctrine?

To justify the warrantless seizure of an item in plain view, the item must not only be in plain view, but its incriminating character must also be immediately apparent.[167]

Are there limitations to the extension of the plain view doctrine?

A truly cursory inspection, involving no more than merely looking at an object already exposed to view, is not a search for Fourth Amendment purposes. However, to physically move an item, for example, to inspect a serial number to determine if the item is stolen, does constitute a search, regardless of the fact that the officer was lawfully present where the item was in plain view.[168]

Must the officer under the "immediately apparent" prong of the doctrine know the items are evidence or contraband?

The "immediately apparent" prong of the plain view doctrine should not be taken to imply that an unduly high degree of certainty by the officer as to the incriminating degree of the evidence is necessary. There is no requirement that the officer "know" that certain items are contraband or evidence of a crime. The seizure of property in plain view involves no invasion of privacy and is presumptively reasonable, assuming that there is probable cause to associate the property with criminal activity.[169]

Under the "plain view" doctrine, a police officer who is lawfully present in a particular place may seize property

---

167. *Id.*
168. Arizona v. Hicks, 480 U.S. 321 (1987).
169. Texas v. Brown, 460 U.S. 730 (1983); Payton v. New York, 445 U.S. 573 (1980).

within his plain view if there is probable cause to associate the property with criminal activity.[170]

The Supreme Court has extended the reasoning of the Plain view doctrine in recent years. Now an officer engaged in a valid *Terry* frisk may seize contraband he detects with his sense of touch so long as the incriminating character of the contraband is immediately apparent.[171]

7. Protective Sweeps

What is a protective sweep and may it be utilized during a search?

A protective sweep is a quick and limited search of a premises incident to an arrest, conducted to protect the safety of police officers or others involved in the search. It is narrowly confined to a cursory-visual inspection of those places in which a person might be hiding. The Fourth Amendment permits a properly limited protective sweep in conjunction with an in-home arrest when the searching officer has a reasonable belief that the area to be swept harbors an individual who poses a danger to those on the arrest scene. The reasonable belief must be based on specific and articulable facts.[172] After the suspect has been arrested and the protective sweep performed, a further warrantless search is not permissible unless justified by exigent circumstances.[173]

---

170. United States v. Silkwood, 893 F.2d 245 (10th Cir. 1989).

171. Minnesota v. Dickerson, 508 U.S. 366, 113 S.Ct. 2130 (1993).

172. Maryland v. Buie, 494 U.S. 325 (1990).

173. Massachusetts v. Lewin, 555 N.E.2d 551 (Mass. 1990).

8. Roadblocks

Is a roadblock a seizure?

The use of a police roadblock to stop the driver of a stolen car constitutes a "seizure" within the meaning of the Fourth Amendment. Should the driver be killed in a collision with the roadblock, a cause of action is stated in that the seizure is unreasonable due to excessive force.[174]

Police may employ highway checkpoint stops as a way of detecting and deterring motorists driving under the influence of intoxicants. Stopping and briefly detaining all motorists passing through such checkpoints is constitutionally reasonable.[175]

9. Curtilage

What is a curtilage?

The "curtilage" concept originated at common law and extends to the area immediately surrounding a dwelling house the same protection as is given to the house itself.[176]

Whether an area constitutes curtilage for Fourth Amendment purposes should be determined based on the following four factors:

(1) the proximity of the area to the home;
(2) whether the area is within an enclosure surrounding the home;
(3) the nature and uses to which the area is put;
(4) the steps taken by the resident to protect the area from observation from passers by. The primary focus is whether the area in question harbors those intimate

---

174. Brower v. County of Inyo, 489 U.S. 593 (1989).
175. Michigan v. Sitz, 496 U.S. 444 (1990).
176. United States v. Dunn, 480 U.S. 294 (1987).

activities associated with domestic life and privacies of the home.[177]

The proximate area around an occupied dwelling in which a person has taken steps to provide for privacy, and which the public would recognize as a reasonable expectation of privacy, is another definition of curtilage.

Does viewing the area inside the curtilage from outside constitute a search?

A police officer's naked-eye observation, from the vantage point of a helicopter circling 400 feet above, of the interior of a partially covered greenhouse in a residential backyard does not constitute a "search" for which a warrant is required.[178] However, even though there is a lessened expectation of privacy in a greenhouse with a clear roof, a helicopter's presence at low altitudes, such as 50 feet, is unreasonable if it presents a hazard to persons and property on the ground.[179]

Is an intrusion upon an open field a search or is it within the curtilage?

The fact that a police officer's intrusion upon an open field is a trespass at common law does not make it a "search" in a constitutional sense.[180]

---

177. Id.
178. Florida v. Riley, 488 U.S. 445 (1989).
179. Pennsylvania v. Oglialoro, 579 A.2d 1288 (Penn. 1990).
180. Oliver v. United States, 466 U.S. 170 (1984).

FIFTH AMENDMENT RIGHTS
OF THE ACCUSED

GRAND JURIES, INTERROGATIONS, CONFESSIONS, AND DOUBLE JEOPARDY

No person shall be held to answer for a capital, or otherwise infamous crime, unless on a presentment or indictment of a Grand Jury, except in cases arising in the land or naval forces, or in the Militia, when in actual service in time of War or public danger; nor shall any person be subject for the same offence to be twice put in jeopardy of life or limb; nor shall be compelled in any criminal case to be a witness against himself, nor be deprived of life, liberty, or property, without due process of law; nor shall private property be taken for public use, without just compensation.[181]

1. Incorporation of Fifth Amendment Guarantees to the States

Under "selective incorporation," virtually all of the Bill of Rights guarantees have been held to apply to the states by the Fourteenth Amendment[182] except the right to indictment by a

---

181. U.S. CONST., AMEND. V.
182. The Court has incorporated the "takings clause," Chicago, Burlington & Quincey Ry. v. Chicago, 166 U.S. 226 (1897); First Amendment protections, Fiske v. Kansas, 274 U.S. 380 (1927); the right to a public trial, In re Oliver, 333 U.S. 257 (1948); Fourth Amendment seizures, Mapp v. Ohio, 367 U.S. 643 (1961); the privilege against self-incrimination, Malloy v. Hogan, 378 U.S. 1 (1964); the right to counsel,

grand jury.[183] In this analysis, the court asks whether the guarantee is "fundamental to the American scheme of justice" so as to be included in the due process clause of the Fourteenth Amendment.[184] When a right applies to a state, it is ordinarily given the same effect as when applied to a federal prosecution.[185]

2. The Grand Jury[186]

What is a grand jury?

The grand jury is an inquisitorial body of citizens established both to insulate the innocent from unfounded charges, and to investigate crimes free from the restraints placed upon

---

Gideon v. Wainwright, 372 U.S. 335 (1963); the right to a speedy trial, Klopfer v. North Carolina, 386 U.S. 213 (1967); the right to confront opposing witnesses, Pointer v. Texas, 380 U.S. 400 (1965); the right to compulsory process to obtain witnesses, Washington v. Texas, 388 U.S. 14 (1967); and double jeopardy, Benton v. Maryland, 395 U.S. 784 (1969).

183. Hurtado v. California, 110 U.S. 516 (1884). *See* Palko v. Connecticut, 302 U.S. 319 (1937) (stating that only those rights "implicit in the concept of ordered liberty" are included in the due process clause of the Fourteenth Amendment). *But cf.* Adamson v. California, 332 U.S. 46 (1947) (Black, J., dissenting) (arguing "fundamental fairness" would include all of the Bill of Rights guarantees).

184. Duncan v. Louisiana, 391 U.S. 145 (1968).

185. *But see* Williams v. Florida, 399 U.S. 78 (1970) (holding six-per son jury does not offend Sixth Amendment); Apodaca v. Oregon, 406 U.S. 404 (1972) (plurality) (allowing nonunananimous verdicts in noncapital cases). Justices and commentators have argued that "total incorporation" of federal rights would necessarily dilute the effect of the right. *See Adamson*, 332 U.S. at 61 (Frankfurter, J., concurring).

186. For a comprehensive treatment of the constitutional and statutory parameters of the federal grand jury, *see* National Lawyers' Guild, Representation of Witnesses Before Federal Grand Juries (3d ed. 1993). Professor Dan S. Murrell is the editor and a author of the Grand Jury Project which produces the service.

the government.[187] The grand jury is an independent body that does not sit to determine guilt or weigh evidence, but to charge crimes. When a grand jury suspects a crime is committed, it may investigate and employ the power of the courts to effect its investigation.Ordinarily, an indictment cannot be challenged for sufficiency of evidence.[188]

What is an indictment?

An indictment is a "True Bill." It merely charges a legally cognizable crime so that the defendant has reasonable opportunity to be apprised of the offense and prepare a defense.[189]

Many states and the Federal Rules of Criminal Procedure[190] provide that a defendant may waive his right to an indictment. This is most frequent when the defendant intends to plead guilty. Failure to waive when the defendant intends to plead guilty is ordinarily a delaying tactic.

What evidence may the grand jury view?

Grand juries are free from the usual procedural restraints placed on government because of its historical nature and common law function.[191] Therefore, grand juries can consider all evidence no matter whether it would be later admissible at trial. An indictment may be based completely on hearsay.[192] A grand jury may consider illegally seized evidence.[193] Refusal to return an indictment by a prior grand jury does not necessarily implicate double jeopardy.[194]

---

187. Costello v. United States, 350 U.S. 359 (1956).
188. *See* United States v. Calandra, 414 U.S. 338 (1974).
189. *See* United State v. Williams, 504 U.S. 36, 112 S. Ct. 1735 (1992).
190. Fed. R. Crim. P 7(a).
191. *See* United States v. Williams, 504 U.S. 36, 112 S. Ct. 1735 (1992).
192. Costello v. United States, 350 U.S. 359 (1956).
193. United States v. Calandra, 414 U.S. 338 (1974).
194. United States v. Thompson, 251 U.S. 407 (1920).

What rights does the witness or target have?

A witness has a limited right against compulsory self-incrimination.[195] If the grand jury, or more appropriately the prosecutor, grants the witness immunity then the witness must testify subject to the sanction of contempt. The purpose of the privilege against self-incrimination is served if the testimony given by the witness is not used in a prosecution of that witness.

A witness may not have counsel present during questioning before the grand jury, but may take notes and consult with counsel outside the grand jury room during questions.

A target has a right to an indictment returned by a constitutionally composed grand jury.[196] This means that the grand jury must represent a fair cross-section of the community racially.[197]

3. Double Jeopardy

What is double jeopardy?

Double jeopardy is the prosecution of the same defendant for the same offense. It must be determined whether in the former prosecution if jeopardy has attached. For jeopardy to have attached, the prosecution must:

(1) be in a court of competent jurisdiction;
(2) be under a valid accusatory pleading; and
(3) reached a point at which the jury has been empaneled and sworn, or when the first witness is sworn if in a bench trial.

---

195. *See* United States v. Dionisio, 410 U.S. 1 (1973).
196. Vasquez v. Hillery, 474 U.S. 254 (1986); 28 U.S.C. §§ 1861 et seq.
197. Taylor v. Louisiana, 419 U.S. 522 (1975).

Successive prosecutions for lesser-included offenses is barred, because the state should be required to bring all applicable charges arising from the same conduct at one proceeding rather than to wear down a defendant with repetitive prosecutions.[198] Furthermore, the Supreme Court has held that Double Jeopardy bars a subsequent prosecution when the defendant's actions were formerly the subject of a non-summary contempt prosecution.[199] It does not matter whether the contempt prosecution was civil or criminal, rather only that the *Blockburger* elements are the same.

What happens if there is a mistrial on prosecution motion?

If, under all the circumstances, there is a "manifest necessity for [taking the case from the jury], or the...ends of justice would otherwise be defeated," then a retrial is not barred.[200] This is so even over a defendant's objection to the mistrial. This determination is within the trial judge's discretion. A judge can declare a mistrial if an impartial verdict cannot be reached, a reversal on appeal is imminent due to procedural error, or the jury is not competent to reach a verdict.[201] A judge may not, however, declare a mistrial to empanel a jury more favorable to the prosecution. If the procedural defect is one that "len[ds] itself to prosecutorial manipulation," then the ends of justice may not be served and a retrial is barred.[202]

What if there is a mistrial on defense motion?

Ordinarily, a defendant may not raise double jeopardy when he has successfully moved for a mistrial, because by

---

198. Harris v. Oklahoma, 433 U.S. 682 (1977).

199. United States v. Dixon, ___ U.S. ___, 113 S. Ct. 2849, 53 CrL 2291 (1993), *overruling* Grady v. Corbin, 495 U.S. 508 (1980).

200. United States v. Perez, 22 U.S (9 Wheat) 579 (1824).

201. *See* Illinois v. Somerville, 410 U.S. 458 (1973).

202. Downum v. United States, 372 U.S. 734 (1963).

doing so he has effectively waived his objection to a retrial.[203] The retention of the double jeopardy claim is stated often as an exception to this rule. Only when the defense can show that the prosecution intended to cause the defense to move for a mistrial can the claim be raised successfully.[204]

Does double jeopardy bar a reprosecution after an acquittal?

A jury verdict acquitting a defendant will always bar a subsequent prosecution. But congress has given the federal government the power to appeal interlocutory dismissals. The government may appeal a dismissal if it is not an adjudication on the merits of the defendant's guilt.[205] Appeals cannot be taken on the sufficiency of evidence to dismiss.[206] The government may not retry a defendant whose conviction is set aside due to errors prejudicial to the prosecution. A retrial may be permissible when the conviction is set aside on collateral attack.[207] A dead-locked jury does not bar reprosecution.

Does double jeopardy bar a reprosecution after a conviction is reversed on appeal?

Appeal of a conviction is a waiver of a later objection to retrial on double jeopardy ground. But the government may not retry a reversal of a conviction on the ground of sufficiency of evidence.[208] This is so because the appellate court has found that the evidence is does not meet the standard set to convict beyond a reasonable doubt. But when a reviewing court reverses on the ground of the weight of the evidence,

---

203. United States v. Dinitz, 424 U.S. 600 (1976).
204. Oregon v. Kennedy, 456 U.S. 667 (1982).
205. United States v. Scott, 437 U.S. 82 (1978).
206. *Id.*
207. United States v. Tateo, 377 U.S. 463 (1964).
208. Burks v. United States, 437 U.S. 1 (1978).

reprosecution is available because the court merely disagrees with the trial court's resolution of conflicting testimony.[209]

If defendant is convicted on a lesser-included offense, he cannot be retried on the higher offense on remand from a reversal.[210]

The prosecution must bring all charges known to it when it brings the initial charge. The government may not seek to "wear a defendant down" or test its case in a prior proceeding. This is compared to the doctrine of res judicata as it would be applied to criminal proceedings.

Can a defendant be retried by a different sovereign?

Under American federalism, the states are sovereign entities apart from the federal government and the government of other states. The subdivisions of a state are not independent sovereigns, however. A defendant cannot be retried on the same offense by the state when there has been a prior prosecution by a municipal division of that state.[211] However, the federal government may retry a defendant after a state prosecution.[212] Most states will bar a subsequent state prosecution following a federal action.

The doctrine of dual sovereignty among states allows two states to prosecute a defendant on the same offense.[213] The defendant has committed offenses against the two states and therefore two separate offenses. This then does not implicate double jeopardy.

209. Tibbs v. Florida, 457 U.S. 31 (1982).
210. Green v. United States, 355 U.S. 184 (1957).
211. Waller v. Florida, 397 U.S. 387 (1970).
212. Bartkus v. Illinois, 359 U.S. 121 (1959).
213. Heath v. Alabama, 474 U.S. 82 (1985).

4. Due Process

To what extent may the police extract a confession?

Due process[214] forbids the use of coerced confessions in a criminal prosecution whether there is actual force[215] or psychological intimidation.[216] Originally, the reasoning behind excluding coerced confessions is that the confession was involuntary and therefore untrustworthy.[217] Eventually, coerced confessions were excluded despite being trustworthy because due process requires an "appropriate procedure before liberty is curtailed."[218] The culmination of the "voluntariness" approach to excluding coerced confessions was in *Spano v. New York*[219] in which the court stated that at least part of the policy behind excluding coerced confessions was to force police to obey the law.

Voluntariness has proved to be a less than reliable standard, however, because the confession that is beaten out of a defendant is to a degree voluntary. But the Court has stated that voluntariness is a question of law to be determined on review of the particular circumstances of the defendant's case to assess whether the defendant's will has been overborne.[220] The courts use a totality of the circumstances approach to determine whether the confession has been extracted by threats of violence, or improper influence.[221]

---

214. The courts may also invoke the supervisory power of the federal courts to invalidate a coerced confession. Mallory v. United States, 354 U.S. 449 (1957).

215. Brown v. Mississippi, 297 U.S. 278 (1936).

216. Ashcraft v. Tennessee, 322 U.S. 143 (1944).

217. *Id.*

218. Watts v. Indiana, 338 U.S. 49 (194); *see also* Rochin v. California, 342 U.S. 165 (1952) (excluding evidence of defendant's stomach being pumped as shocking the judicial conscience).

219. 360 U.S. 315 (1959).

220. Miller v. Fenton, 474 U.S. 104 (1985); *see also* Arizona v. Fulminante, 499 U.S. 279 (1991).

221. Spano v. New York, 360 U.S. 315 (1959).

Although the voluntariness due process standard applies to police practices, if a private party coerces a confession, due process will not exclude it absent some state action.[222]

The Privilege Against Self-Incrimination

Does the Fifth Amendment privilege against self-incrimination apply to a coerced state confession?

The Court has held the privilege against self-incrimination applicable to the states through the Fourteenth Amendment.[223] The same standard was applied to state confessions as to federal confessions, that is the voluntariness standard.[224] The privilege against self-incrimination is a personal testimonial privilege and may not be asserted on behalf of another or for nontestimonial evidence.

In *Miranda v. Arizona*,[225] the Court held that any statement by a criminal defendant during a custodial interrogation is inadmissible as substantive evidence of guilt unless the state can show that procedural safeguards were followed to protect the defendant's privilege against self-incrimination. The prosecution can, however, impeach a witness with inadmissible statements.[226] These safeguards must be fully effective to insure that the Fifth Amendment is not offended. The Court announced a laundry list of interests the state must respect. These include the following:

1. The right to be silent.
2. Defendant's knowledge of the failure to remain silent.

---

222. Colorado v. Connelly, 479 U.S. 157 (1986).
223. Malloy v. Hogan, 378 U.S. 1 (1964).
224. *Id.*; *see also* Bram v. United States, 168 U.S. 532 (1897).
225. 384 U.S. 436 (1966).
226. Michigan v. Harvey, 494 U.S. 344 (1990).

3. Defendant's knowledge of the right to have counsel present during questioning.[227]
4. Defendant's knowledge that counsel will be provided if necessary if he or she cannot afford counsel.

What are the policies behind the Miranda decision?

A custodial interrogation carries with it the "badge of intimidation" and subjects an accused to forms of persuasion that cannot be viewed "otherwise than [a] compulsion to speak." Such a situation preys on the weaknesses of individuals.

Confessions are not so valuable a law enforcement tool as to allow a balance of interests to determine if and when a violation of the Fifth Amendment occurs.

The Fifth Amendment marks "the hallmark of our democracy" and requires the government to carry the entire burden of the prosecution.

Can fruits of statements made in violation of Miranda be used against an accused?

Miranda does not prevent the fruits of admissions prior to the warnings from being used.[228] Rather, *Miranda* is a prophylactic safeguard to provide a practical reinforcement of the privilege against self-incrimination. Furthermore, the Court has held that some exceptions to the requirement of *Miranda* exist. *Miranda* does not confer substantive rights, and a violation of its mandate does not necessarily require exclusion of the statements. If the defendant responds to questions posed by the police in the interest of public safety, then these cannot be excluded for failure to give the prophylactic warnings.[229]

---

227. This is known as the "Miranda right to counsel" because the Sixth Amendment right to counsel does not apply until formal proceedings commence, or a critical stage—an indictment is handed up.

228. Michigan v. Tucker, 417 U.S. 433 (1974).

229. New York v. Quarles, 467 U.S. 649 (1984).

Are there exceptions to the Miranda requirement?

Because *Miranda* does not confer rights, if the police obtain a statement without the warnings and subsequently obtain the same statement with the warnings, the second proper statement may be used.[230]

Miranda warnings are not required when a suspect is unaware he is speaking to a law enforcement officer.[231]

Miranda may not apply to routine booking questions such as name and age, but will only apply if the police ask incriminating questions.

Can the defendant waive his Miranda rights?

A defendant can waive his *Miranda* rights if the prosecution shows that the waiver was knowing, voluntary, and intelligent. The prosecution must show a waiver by a preponderance standard.[232] A waiver can be implied, but it will not be presumed from a defendant's silence.[233] A waiver must be the product of deliberate choice, not from coercion or deception,[234] and a waiver is invalid if the police used less that appropriate means to obtain it. The standard for an effective waiver is merely that the defendant have a rational understanding of the proceedings pending against him and a reasonable ability to assist in his defense.[235]

Once a defendant has chosen to remain silent[236] or requested counsel[237] the interrogation must cease. However, if the

---

230. Oregon v. Elstad, 470 U.S. 298 (1985).
231. Illinois v. Perkins, 496 U.S. 292 (1987).
232. Colorado v. Connelly, 479 U.S. 157 (1986).
233. Moran v. Burbine, 475 U.S. 412 (1086).
234. Colorado v. Connelly, 479 U.S. 157 (1986).
235. Godinez v. Moran, ___ U.S. ___, 113 S. Ct. 2680; 53 CrL 2240 (1993); *see also* Dusky v. United States, 362 U.S. 402 (1960) (defendant must make a "reasoned choice" to plead guilty).
236. Michigan v. Mosely, 423 U.S. 96 (1975).
237. Edwards v. Arizona, 451 U.S. 477 (1981).

police scrupulously honor the defendant's request, they may initiate further questioning. Furthermore, if the defendant initiates further communication, the police may continue the interrogation.

What is an interrogation?

An interrogation is not only the formal custodial questioning, but also when its functional equivalent occurs. *Miranda* warnings should be given when the police reasonably should know that their questions will elicit an incriminating response.[238] This focuses on the perceptions of the suspect.

When is a defendant in custody?

A defendant is in custody for *Miranda* purposes when he is actually in custody or is deprived of his freedom in any significant way. A suspect arrested for a traffic violation is entitled to *Miranda* warnings. The question is whether a reasonable person in the defendant's circumstances would view the situation as having his freedom curtailed.[239] *Miranda* is not limited only to those interrogations in the police station.[240]

---

238. Rhode Island v. Innis, 446 U.S. 291 (1980).
239. Berkmer v. McCarty, 468 U.S. 420 (1984).
240. California v. Beheler, 463 U.S. 1121 (1983).

Also of interest from Carolina Academic Press...

Constitutional Law and Liability Series for Law Enforcement Officers

Constitutional Law and Liability for Agents, Deputies and Police Officers
Dan S. Murrell and William O. Dwyer

A quick and handy reference for law enforcement officers on how the Constitution, as interpreted through various court decisions, influences their contacts with the public. The book presents a sound framework against which the practice of law enforcement may be measured. It is not meant to be a complete list of "Do's and Don'ts," because various state laws and local regulations, as well as agency guidelines and procedures, may also have a bearing on the breadth of enforcement authority given to police officers. Therefore, where more restrictive guidelines are in place, the reader is cautioned to make a note of them.

1992 • paperback • 192 pp • $15.00

Constitutional Law and Liability for Public-Sector Police
Airports, Port Authorities, Public Medical Facilities, Public Colleges and Universities
Dan S. Murrell and William O. Dwyer

This book, along with basic constitutional law for law enforcement officers, addresses issues, including liability, that pertain specifically to this specialized branch of policing. The general rules are essentially the same as they would be for any police officer, yet these institutional police operate in a unique environment that sometimes makes the application of case law difficult and confusing, but may also give them more latitude in policing.

1992 • paperback • 198 pp • $15.00

Constitutional Law and Liability for Park Law Enforcement Officers
Third Edition
Dan S. Murrell and William O. Dwyer

An update of the 1990 version with an extensive section on liability and coverage of the most recent court cases, this is a comprehensive reference for park law enforcement officers. "Consisting of fourteen sections, this very informative text covers all areas of constitutional law... [It] not only explains the various aspects of the law, but also provides answers to some of the questions most frequently asked by park rangers... Overall, this book is an excellent guide, and I feel a "must" for all federal and state park law enforcement officers." *RANGER: The Journal of the Association of National Park Rangers*

1991 • paperback • 192 pp • $15.00

Investigative Discourse Analysis
Statements, Letters and Transcripts
Don Rabon

Too often investigators from all areas and fields consider written statements, transcripts of interviews and interrogations, and letters as mere pieces of paper to be filed. They are only useful at face value — as simple records, sworn statements, archives. In Investigative Discourse Analysis, Don Rabon demonstrates that these files can be put to work. These files can mean much more if the investigator uses proven techniques to move beyond the archive.

These files are analogous to a crime scene. To the uninitiated, the crime scene might look like just an ordinary room. To the trained eye, however, there can be evidence for follow-up everywhere. This book introduces techniques for discourse analysis, in which a statement can be examined for more information than that available to the untrained eye.

These techniques lead the investigator to the sensitive areas of the statement or transcript where there might be deception. Armed with indications of the intent to falsify or conceal, the investigator can then focus the investigation on the heart of the deception. Follow-up questions and further investigation can be planned and executed.

1994 • paperback • 192 pp • $14.95

Interviewing and Interrogation
Don Rabon

The goal in an interrogation, or in any situation where a person with information might be uncooperative, is to effect a transition in willingness — ethically and legally. A successful interrogation becomes, in fact, an interview when the subject grows willing to yield details freely and honestly. In order to initiate this transition, the interrogator/interviewer must understand the subject's motivation, the basics of effective inquiry, and techniques of ethical and legal persuasion. They must also recognize the process by which those interviewed can deceive — and how deception can be detected. This book demonstrates to interviewers the fundamentals of effective inquiry.

The text is divided into six chapters. Each chapter is organized around the concept of process, which indicates that there is a way to proceed and that the procedure involves specific steps. Each of the first five chapters is followed by a series of questions and is accompanied by an appendix containing exercises designed to reinforce the concepts contained in the chapter. The sixth chapter provides an opportunity to apply the inquiry and persuasion techniques developed in previous chapters to the transcript of an actual interview.

1992 • paperback • 212 pp • $14.95